WHAT EVANGELICALS BELIEVE

What Evangelicals Believe

Edited by
Andrew Anderson

Bible Churches
growing together

CROSSWAY BOOKS

ISBN 1 85684 021 2

Typeset by Medcalf Type Ltd, Bicester, Oxon
Printed in Great Britain for Crossway Books, Kingfisher House,
7 High Green, Great Shelford, Cambridge by
Cox & Wyman Ltd, Cardiff Road, Reading

Contents

Preface

Evangelical Christians believe that the Bible is the word of God and so they believe in the great truths that the Bible teaches. They are happy to set out what they believe in doctrinal statements which affirm essential truth and act as a fence against error.

This book is geared to the doctrinal basis of the Fellowship of Independent Evangelical Churches, which has the title, *What We Believe*. But the statement is not limited to one grouping of evangelicals. It seeks to express for our day the unchangeable truths of historic, biblical Christianity – the faith that is shared and proclaimed by all who are truly evangelical.

So here is a short commentary on the *What We Believe* statement.

It was written by the members of the Theological Committee of FIEC: Andrew Anderson, Paul Brown, Brian Edwards, David Middleton, Colin Smith and Jonathan Stephen.

We hope that this book may be, for some, a key to open up the Christian faith to them; for others, a useful summary to draw together in a more coherent way the things they believe; and, for all who read it, a stimulus to going further and seeking to know more.

What We Believe

1. God
There is one God, who exists eternally in three distinct but equal persons: the Father, the Son and the Holy Spirit. God is unchangeable in his holiness, justice, wisdom and love. He is the almighty Creator, Saviour and Judge who sustains and governs all things according to his sovereign will for his own glory.

2. The Bible
God has revealed himself in the Bible, which consists of the Old and New Testaments alone. Every word was inspired by God through human authors, so that the Bible as originally given is in its entirety the word of God, without error and fully reliable in fact and doctrine. The Bible alone speaks with final authority and is always sufficient for all matters of belief and practice.

3. The Human Race
All men and women, being created in the image of God, have inherent and equal dignity and worth. Their greatest purpose is to obey, worship and love God. As a result of the fall of our first parents, every aspect of human nature has been corrupted and all men and

1

women are without spiritual life, guilty sinners and hostile to God. Every person is therefore under the just condemnation of God and needs to be born again, forgiven and reconciled to God in order to know and please him.

4. The Lord Jesus Christ

The Lord Jesus Christ is fully God and fully man. He was conceived by the Holy Spirit, born of a virgin, and lived a sinless life in obedience to the Father. He taught with authority and all his words are true. On the cross he died in the place of sinners, bearing God's punishment for their sin, redeeming them by his blood. He rose from the dead and in his resurrection body ascended into heaven where he is exalted as Lord of all. He intercedes for his people in the presence of the Father.

5. Salvation

Salvation is entirely a work of God's grace and cannot be earned or deserved. It has been accomplished by the Lord Jesus Christ and is offered to all in the gospel. God in his love forgives sinners whom he calls, granting them repentance and faith. All who believe in Christ are justified by faith alone, adopted into the family of God and receive eternal life.

6. The Holy Spirit

The Holy Spirit has been sent from heaven to glorify Christ and to apply his work of salvation. He convicts sinners, imparts spiritual life and gives a true understanding of the Scriptures. He indwells all believers, brings assurance of salvation and produces increasing likeness to Christ. He builds up the church and empowers its members for worship, service and mission.

7. The Church

The universal church is the body of which Christ is the head and to which all who are saved belong. It is made visible in local churches, which are congregations of believers who are committed to each other for the worship of God, the preaching of the word, the administering of baptism and the Lord's Supper, for pastoral care and discipline, and for evangelism. The unity of the body of Christ is expressed within and between churches by mutual love, care and encouragement. True fellowship between churches exists only where they are faithful to the gospel.

8. Baptism and the Lord's Supper

Baptism and the Lord's Supper have been given to the churches by Christ as visible signs of the gospel. Baptism is a symbol of union with Christ and entry into his church but does not impart spiritual life. The Lord's Supper is a commemoration of Christ's sacrifice offered once for all and involves no change in the bread and wine. All its blessings are received by faith.

9. The Future

The Lord Jesus Christ will return in glory. He will raise the dead and judge the world in righteousness. The wicked will be sent to eternal punishment and the righteous will be welcomed into a life of eternal joy in fellowship with God. God will make all things new and will be glorified for ever.

1

About God

There is one God, who exists eternally in three distinct but equal persons: the Father, the Son and the Holy Spirit. God is unchangeable in his holiness, justice, wisdom and love. He is the almighty Creator, Saviour and Judge who sustains and governs all things according to his sovereign will for his own glory.

*   *   *

Is there a God? Does he really exist? Sooner or later discussions about religion get back to the ultimate question. But the Bible nowhere argues the case for the existence of God. Its very first words simply state: 'In the beginning God . . .' (Gen 1:1). It is as if God were saying, 'I am here.'

Right from its start the Bible confronts us with the fact that God exists, that he made the world, and that we are all accountable to him. So when we state what we as Christians believe we must begin by saying something about God.

Something . . . not everything! God is so great and so wonderful that the most brilliant mind could never grasp all that there is to know about him. Nevertheless,

God has revealed all that we need to know about him. He has done so in the world about us (nature) and much more fully in the book he has given us (Scripture). What does the Bible say about God?

The Bible asserts that *there is one God* (Deut 6:4). At different times and in various parts of the world people have believed in all sorts of gods, but these are all false gods. There is only one true and living God (Is 44:6; 45:6; 1 Thess 1:9). And he *exists eternally*. There never was a time in the past when the true and living God did not exist and there will never be a time in the future when he will cease to be (Ps 90:2).

Some people think of God as a mystic force or just a vague influence for good. But although he is spirit (Jn 4:24) he is someone who knows us and whom it is possible for us to know (Exod 3:14; 1 Jn 1:3).

Actually, God is three persons. The word 'Trinity' (triunity) is not found in the Bible, but it is a useful word to sum up the teaching of the Scriptures that God is one God *who exists eternally in three distinct but equal persons: the Father, the Son and the Holy Spirit.*

There are hints of the doctrine of the Trinity in the Old Testament, the first way back in that very first chapter of the Bible. The word that is used there for God, Elohim, isn't singular, it's plural, and you will notice that God says, 'Let us make . . .' (Gen 1:26). When we come to the New Testament the idea becomes clearer. As good Jews the disciples of Jesus were strong believers that there is one God but they came to believe that Jesus himself was God, which is what he certainly claimed to be (Jn 10:30,33). And Jesus told them that he would send 'another Counsellor', the Holy Spirit (Jn 14:16 – 17). The disciples and the Christian church had to come to terms with the fact that God is more mysterious and more

6

wonderful than they had ever imagined. He is one in essence, yet he is three persons.

Jesus commissioned his followers to go and make disciples of all nations and commanded that these should be baptised 'in the name [one name because there is one God] of the Father and of the Son and of the Holy Spirit' (three persons (Mt 28:18 – 20). Paul prayed for the early Christians in Corinth in the now-familiar words, 'May the grace of the Lord Jesus Christ, and the love of God, and the fellowship of the Holy Spirit be with you all' (2 Cor 13:14). His prayer was to the one God, but he asked the blessing of the three persons.

We need to avoid either thinking of God as a single person or talking as if there were three gods. There is one God and he is three distinct and equal persons. The Lord Jesus is God yet he is distinct from the Father. The Holy Spirit is God yet he is distinct from both the Father and the Son. Nevertheless, the Father, the Son and the Holy Spirit are equally God (Jn 16:7 – 15; 20:21 – 22; Eph 2:18; 1 Pet 1:2).

Of course, the teaching that God is one God yet three persons is very hard to understand. Perhaps it is good for us to have to admit that we find it hard. After all, our finite minds could never understand the infinite God completely. There is a mystery about the nature of God and we must humbly accept that it is so.

What else does the Bible say about God?

It says that *God is unchangeable*. How different he is from us! Our lives are constantly subject to change: circumstances change, people around us change and so do our moods. But God does not change in any way (Jas 1:17). He is not thrown by circumstances nor does he vary at all. He says, 'I the Lord do not change' (Mal 3:6).

We would have to compile a very long list of the

characteristics of God if we were to try to describe him fully. But four of the most important words that give some description of his nature are *holiness, justice, wisdom* and *love*. And remember none of these will ever change, for God will never change.

God is holy: he is utterly pure in all his motives, in all his thoughts, in all his words and in all his deeds (Exod 15:11; Is 40:25). He is just: everything he does is right, he treats people with complete impartiality, and when he judges the world the judgement will be absolutely fair (Rom 2:11; Ps 96:13). God is wise: he knows everything and all he does shows his wisdom (Dan 2:22–23; Rom 11:33–36). He is loving: incredibly so when you think how he loves people who have not loved him (1 Jn 4:8–10).

God is *the almighty Creator*. By his powerful word the universe was made and so was the planet earth and man who lives on it. God did not have to create anything; he chose to do so, and he created everything out of nothing. He did not work on what was there, because nothing was there but him (Gen 1–2; Heb 11:3).

God is *the Saviour*. We will have to look in some detail at the grim reality that men and women have rebelled against their Creator. But God has a marvellous way of saving sinners. No one can ever save himself: if a sinner is to be saved God must save him (Tit 3:4–7; Rev 7:9–10).

God is *the Judge*. All men must meet their Maker one day. 'Man is destined to die once, and after that to face judgment' (Heb 9:27). No one will be able to cancel that appointment or avoid answering to God for the life he has lived in God's world. We all have to give an account to him (Rom 14:12; Rev 20:11–15).

The world holds together and we breathe in every

breath only because God provides for his creation. He *sustains all things* (Heb 1:3; Job 12:10). And despite all appearance to the contrary, God *governs all things according to his sovereign will for his own glory*.

He rules over all and nothing lies outside his kingly control (Ps 103:19; Dan 4:34–35). He grants many good things to happen, and in his goodness he checks sin. Even though there is much evil in the world, God is so great and so good he can turn evil to work for the ultimate good (Gen 50:20 and Acts 2:23 give examples). That does not justify sin in any way but it shows how wonderful God is that he is able to work everything without exception for his own glory (Eph 1:11–12).

How should we feel about the God who is revealed like this in the Bible? Isaiah felt small and sinful when he saw something of the majesty and the moral purity of God (Is 6:1–8). Should we not feel small when we realise how great God is and should we not feel sinful too, when we think of how perfect he is? Above all, should we not praise and worship him?

Study Questions

1. How would you try to convince a friend who has doubts about the existence of God that God really does exist?
2. Find as many references as you can from the New Testament that show that the one God is three persons.
3. What part does each person in the Trinity, the Father, the Son and the Holy Spirit, play in the salvation of sinners? Ephesians 1:3–14 is one place to look.
4. How can God be holy, just, wise and loving when there is so much suffering in the world?
5. We have talked about what God is like and what God does. Make a list of things we have said that should make us praise and worship him.

2

About the Bible

God has revealed himself in the Bible, which consists of the Old and New Testaments alone. Every word was inspired by God through human authors, so that the Bible as originally given is in its entirety the word of God, without error and fully reliable in fact and doctrine. The Bible alone speaks with final authority and is always sufficient for all matters of belief and practice.

*　　*　　*

God made us and we would therefore expect him to tell us about himself and what he requires of us; without a clear revelation from God we would have no voice of authority to guide us through life. In this hope we are not disappointed because *God has revealed himself in the Bible* (Jn 5:39; Heb 1:1). This is the best and most important thing about the Bible.

The Bible is not first of all God giving us rules and regulations, or describing our sin and helplessness; it is God telling us about himself. Since the Fall, man has misread the evidence of God in nature (Acts 14:17–18; Rom 1:18–20) and so he worships false gods and idols (Rom 1:21–23). Our minds are clouded by sin and if

God had not revealed himself we would never be able to know him. Our best and clearest understanding of who God is comes through the Bible. In the Bible we read of his law (his rules and man's failure to keep them) and his gospel (his Son and the way we can be saved). All this tells us about the kind of God he is.

There are many religious books in the world but only one that comes from God and truthfully reveals God to us: *the Bible which consists of the Old and New Testaments alone*. The Bible is in two parts. There are thirty-nine books in the Old Testament and twenty-seven in the New Testament. The word 'testament' means a covenant or promise made by God. The Old Testament takes us up to 400 years before the birth of Christ and tells us about creation, God's choice of the Jews as his special people and about his laws for them and how they were to worship him. Some of it also looks forward to the coming of Jesus Christ. It is 'old' because it was preparing the way for the new and better promises in Jesus Christ (Lk 24:27; Heb 9:15).

The New Testament tells us about the birth, life, death and resurrection of Jesus Christ and the life and growth of the first-century Christian church. Some of it also tells us about the future. But remember, all this is God revealing himself.

In the 400 years between the close of the Old Testament and the start of the New Testament, no Bible book was written. Some religious books were written which people have tried to add to the Bible; together these books are called 'The Apocrypha', but Christ and his apostles did not recognise them as God's word and so neither do we. There are no other Bible books outside of the Old and New Testaments.

Because we know God is our almighty creator, we expect him to speak to us in a way that is reliable and true (Ps 119:160; Tit 1:2). It would not be sufficient to have a general idea of what God wanted to say or just the gist of his meaning. When God used human writers to write down the Bible books (and about forty writers were involved over a period of 1,500 years) the Holy Spirit made sure that no error crept into their writing; so they recorded exactly what God wanted them to say and exactly how he wanted them to say it, in their own culture, style and language (2 Tim 3:16; 2 Pet 1:20–21; 1 Cor 2:13). In this way *every word was inspired by God through human authors*.

God used men so that the Bible would be a human book; but his Holy Spirit ensured that *the Bible as originally given is in its entirety the word of God*. Of course we no longer have the original handwritten copies of Moses' first five books of the Bible or of Isaiah's prophecy, or of Paul's New Testament letters, or of any other part of the Bible. The best we have are copies that were themselves the result of a long process of copying. In the process, here and there small errors have crept in but, as one scholar has said, not one thousandth part of our Bible is affected by this; and certainly not one Christian doctrine is affected by this. God has preserved for us so many ancient copies of Bible books that by comparing them, we can learn how incredibly alike they are and therefore how accurate the copying is. We need have no doubt that our Bible today is God's word.

Some people say that because they were human writers there must be mistakes everywhere. Others believe that mistakes are limited to things like points of history and geography, dates and numbers, but are not present where the Bible speaks about the big issues of salvation and the character of God.

Such views fail to understand that you cannot separate history and doctrine. For example, Paul's whole argument in 1 Corinthians 15 is that the security of our salvation depends upon the historical fact of Christ's resurrection. And both Peter and John lay an important stress on the fact that they were eye-witnesses of the history they record (2 Pet 1:16 – 18; 1 Jn 1:1 – 3). Besides, these views fail also to appreciate that inspiration means that all Scripture comes from God as the Author; the Bible is therefore 'God-breathed' (2 Tim 3:16) and every word of it is true (Prov 30:5). We can rely on every part of the Bible: it is all *without error and fully reliable in fact and doctrine*.

At the time of the Reformation in the sixteenth century the great debate over Scripture was whether popes, councils and the church fathers had more authority than the Bible. The Reformers claimed that *the Bible alone speaks with final authority*. We may talk of God speaking to us through the preacher's message, or of men speaking or writing with a voice of authority; and there is a sense in which both of these claims may be true. But though God speaks to us like this, the final authority must always be the Bible. The Bible has a unique authority that cannot be claimed for anything or anyone else (Col 2:8). It is only about Scripture that we can claim with absolute certainty that God has put his words in the mind of the writer (Jer 1:9; Amos 3:8; Zech 7:12; 1 Cor 2:13; 1 Thess 2:13; 2 Pet 3:2).

The Bible is always sufficient for all matters of belief and practice. Books written by men are dated and of passing value; the Bible, on the other hand, is of constant value. It alone is all we need to tell us what we should believe about God and salvation, and its principles are a sufficient guide for the way we should live. We need no other words from God for our belief and practice; there can be no more Bible (Deut 4:2; Prov 30:5–6; Jude 3; Rev 22:18–19).

Study Questions

1. List as many reasons as you can why it is important to believe in a Bible without any error.
2. How do we know that God has no more Bible beyond the sixty-six books?
3. What reasons do people use to try and disprove the accuracy of the Bible? Briefly, how would you counter these arguments?
4. Read carefully 2 Peter 1:16–21. What do these verses teach us about the reliability of Scripture?
5. Put in your own words what we mean when we say that the Bible is 'sufficient'.

3

About the Human Race

All men and women, being created in the image of God, have inherent and equal dignity and worth. Their greatest purpose is to obey, worship and love God. As a result of the fall of our first parents, every aspect of human nature has been corrupted and all men and women are without spiritual life, guilty sinners and hostile to God. Every person is therefore under the just condemnation of God and needs to be born again, forgiven and reconciled to God in order to know and please him.

*   *   *

It is surprising how little preaching and teaching we hear about the human race and human nature. Surprising, because the Bible itself has so much to say. The Bible presents us with a clear, convincing but radical view of humanity, which is unlike that of any other religion or philosophy.

The foundation for understanding human nature is that *all men and women* are *created in the image of God*. This is true not only for the first man and woman (Gen 1:26–27) and for the human race as a whole (Ps 8:4–5), but also for each individual, for you and me (Ps 139:13 – 14). Bible-believing Christians differ in the way they relate the truth of creation to the theories of evolution, but the fundamental fact is inescapable: the human race and each individual in it is created by God.

While Genesis 1 does not define in detail the *image of God*, it can be clearly seen from Genesis 2 that the first man and woman reflected the nature of God as being spiritual, moral, rational and free. Thus God and mankind could enjoy the highest degree of personal communion. It is equally obvious that they were created righteous and free from sin (Eccles 7:29).

If we are, each one of us, created in the image of God then it is sure that we *have inherent and equal dignity and worth*, and that this remains true in spite of the Fall (Jas 3:9; Mt 10:31; 12:12; Mk 8:36 – 37). No one race or colour of skin is superior to any other in God's sight (Acts 10:34 – 35; 17:26; Rom 2:11). Racism, sexism, and all forms of discrimination and exploitation, are contrary to God's plan of creation.

We need immediately to add to this that God created mankind with an amazingly high purpose. That purpose is not only to care for God's earthly creation (Gen 1:28), but supremely and uniquely *to obey, worship and love God* (Exod 19:5; Ps 86:9; Mt 22:37; 1 Cor 10:31).

This Christian view of human nature as having a divine origin and having such a high dignity and purpose must be held on to firmly over against views that reduce human beings to mere machines or animals. In fact it is only when we consider the marvel of unfallen humanity that we can evaluate the consequences of the Fall, and can sense the paradox of men and women today as being at the same time gloriously created, yet tragically fallen.

The Bible teaches that *as a result of the fall of our first*

parents, every aspect of human nature has been corrupted. Genesis
1 and 2 show mankind to be originally righteous. Genesis
3 records the first sin against God as an historical event.
But what is significant is that the effect of that first sin
was not only upon Adam and Eve, but also upon the
whole subsequent human race. Human nature has been
changed. We are a fallen race (Rom 5:12–19). The Bible
does not attempt to explain the 'mechanics' of the
transmission of sin down through human history. But
we can say that Adam was both the natural and 'official'
head and representative of mankind, so that we are all
involved in his defeat and fall from innocence.

Every aspect of human nature had been corrupted in some
way: the body (Rom 8:10), the mind (Eph 4:17–18),
the heart (Jer 17:9), the conscience (Tit 1:15), the will
(Rom 7:18–19). Our physical, intellectual, emotional
and moral life is all now distorted by sin.

Scripture even teaches us that *all men and women are
without spiritual life* (Eph 2:1), so that we cannot initiate
any spiritual movement towards God without his grace.
We are *guilty sinners* (Ps 51:5; Rom 3:19–20). We are
hostile to God (Rom 8:7; Jn 3:19), so that we are opposed
to his good laws and his claims upon our lives.

None of this takes away from the fact that every
individual is accountable to God and is personally
responsible for his or her own sins (Jas 1:14).
Nevertheless, if we are to understand how deep the work
of salvation needs to go, we have to face the fact that
none of us enters life with the original uncorrupted
innocence of our first parents, but with a human nature
already disabled by sin and bereft of real spiritual life.
It is on this sad foundation that we build our personal
sin and failure.

The biblical teaching of the Fall and its consequences

for the whole human race has been constantly attacked. But solemn as this teaching is, nothing else does justice to the picture that the Bible gives us of human nature, and nothing else so convincingly explains the contradictions we observe in human life every day. Unaided reason is unable to comprehend such truths (1 Cor 2:14), but they are true to Scripture and true to experience.

Quite apart from the way sin affects human nature, and thus character and conduct, it is clearly taught in the Bible that *every person is under the just condemnation of God*. God, as Judge of all, cannot but pronounce sinners guilty and under his judgement, and that judgement must inevitably fall on them, unless the process is interrupted by God's own grace (Rom 1:18; Eph 2:3).

Once again, these are truths that are attacked, eroded or avoided altogether in the present day, but unless we are convinced of them we will fail to appreciate the greatness of the salvation we have in Jesus Christ.

It is because the human dilemma is so intense and deep rooted that the need of every person is *to be born again, forgiven and reconciled to God in order to know and please him* (Jn 3:3, 5–8; Rom 4:7; 2 Cor 5:18–19; Eph 1:7). Although the expression 'born again' has been devalued in contemporary usage, this must not disguise the fact that every human being needs not only the forgiveness of specific sins, but a profound life-giving, life-changing work of God's Spirit that Jesus called new birth.

This is not the end of the story. In Jesus Christ as the new Adam, Christians do not have their humanity refined away, or lost in God, but fulfilled, and ultimately transformed and glorified as we share the likeness of God's perfect Man, our Lord and Saviour Jesus Christ.

Study Questions

1. What should it mean to us to know that we are God's creatures, made in his image, rather than accidents of evolution?
2. What aspects of the image of God in Adam can be discovered from the events of Genesis 2?
3. How can we counter the claim that the doctrine of 'original sin' is somehow unjust?
4. What evidence do you see for men and women being hostile to God?
5. Why do sinners need to be born again?

4

About the Lord Jesus Christ

The Lord Jesus Christ is fully God and fully man. He was conceived by the Holy Spirit, born of a virgin, and lived a sinless life in obedience to the Father. He taught with authority and all his words are true. On the cross he died in the place of sinners, bearing God's punishment for their sin, redeeming them by his blood. He rose from the dead and in his resurrection body ascended into heaven where he is exalted as Lord of all. He intercedes for his people in the presence of the Father.

*   *   *

There is nothing that brings greater joy to a Christian than to consider the Lord Jesus Christ, both who he is and what he has done (Heb 3:1; 12:1–3). To fix our eyes on the One who is our Saviour and our Lord strengthens our faith, warms our hearts and encourages us in perseverance and service.

The Bible makes it absolutely clear that *the Lord Jesus Christ is fully God and fully man*. In his one person two distinct natures, divine and human, are inseparably joined together, but not combined or mixed in any way. We are left in no doubt about his full deity:

— he is called God (Jn 1:1; Heb 1:8; Is 9:6; 1 Jn 5:20);
— verses which refer to the Lord (Jehovah) in the Old
  Testament are applied to him (Lk 1:76; 3:4 [Is 40:3];
  Phil 2:10–11 [Is 45:18,23]);
— he takes the name I AM to himself (Jn 8:58–59);
— he is described in terms which can only apply to God
  (all-knowing—Jn 2:25; eternal—Rev 22:13;
  unchangeable—Heb 13:8);
— he does in his own name things which only God can
  do (Jn 1:3; 6:4–14; 11:43–44);
— we are to worship him (Jn 20:28; Mt 28:17; Rev
  1:5–6).

While never ceasing to be fully God he also became
fully man (Jn 1:14); *he was conceived by the Holy Spirit,
born of a virgin.* His incarnation, as his taking human
nature is usually called, is a great mystery to us (1 Tim
3:16), and it took place by means of a miracle. Jesus
had no human father but derived his human nature
from his mother Mary. She conceived him while she
was still a virgin (Mt 1:18–23; Lk 1:27,34), as the result
of a special act of the Holy Spirit upon her body (Lk
1:35; Mt 1:18).

So he became, and remains, fully man:

— He has a human body, a human soul, a human will,
  a human mind, human emotions; he was made like
  us in every way (Heb 2:14,17);
— He grew up in this world from childhood to manhood,
  he knew family life and friendship, hunger and thirst,
  weariness and loneliness, grief but also gladness (Lk
  2:41–52; Mt 4:2; Jn 19:28; 4:6; Mt 26:40; Jn
  11:3,5,35; Lk 10:21);
— He tasted death in all its bitterness (Heb 2:9).

He knows the whole range of human experiences and is able to sympathise with us fully in all that we pass through, and help us when we call upon him (Heb 2:18; 4:15). Yet in one respect he was not like us at all. Throughout his earthly life, and in spite of every temptation, he lived a sinless life in obedience to the Father (Heb 4:15; 7:26; Jn 17:4).

The Gospels that tell us of the events of his life and death also record for us many of the things that he said. He spoke as no one had ever spoken before (Jn 7:46). Unlike the Jewish synagogue teachers of the day, who constantly referred to traditional interpretations when they expounded the Old Testament, *he taught with authority*. It is not surprising that this was what people noted most about his teaching ministry (Mt 7:28 – 29), for he only taught what the Father had given him to say (Jn 7:16 – 17; 8:26 – 28). *All his words are true*; we must listen carefully to him and do what he says (Mt 17:5; 7:24 – 27; 12:46 – 50).

The day came when he died; crucified. Even his death, awful as it was, was all part of the plan of God for him— and for us (Acts 2:23; 4:27 – 28)! *On the cross he died in the place of sinners*. This was pictured by the sacrifices of the Old Testament in which animals were substituted for sinful people and killed, bearing sins which had been placed upon them (Lev 1:4). Jesus became the sustitute for sinners and died, *bearing God's punishment for their sin* (Is 53:4 – 6; Jn 1:29; 1 Cor 15:3; 1 Pet 2:24). The justice of God demands the death of the sinner (Rom 6:23; Ezek 18:20), but the love of God has provided his Son to die instead (Rom 5:8). At the cross justice and love meet together (see Ps 85:10), and both are seen at their fullest expression.

What Jesus Christ has done for us by his death is

24

described in various ways in the Bible, and different words are used to bring out the full significance of his salvation. One of these words is 'redemption', which means deliverance by the payment of a price. In the ancient world this word was often used of slaves being set free. They were redeemed, set free, because a price had been paid. All Christians were once slaves to sin (Jn 8:34), but Jesus Christ has set them free (Jn 8:36), *redeeming them by his blood*. The word 'blood' also has a special meaning in the Bible. Life is in the blood (Lev 17:11,14), so the shedding of blood refers to life violently taken away (Gen 9:6; 4:10 – 11). Moreover, God gave the blood of animals to be used in sacrifices as the ransom price (Lev 17:11—"to make atonement" literally means "pay a ransom"). The violent shedding of the blood of Christ in death is the price by which we are set free from sin and all its consequences (Eph 1:7; 1 Pet 1:18 – 19; Gal 3:13; Mt 20:28). We are bought with a price; and what a price! We are not our own any longer; we are God's and we must glorify him with our bodies (1 Cor 6:19 – 20).

Jesus Christ died—but on the third day *he rose from the dead*. The Father had accepted his sacrifice, and to demonstrate that the price of sin had been paid once and for ever, Jesus was raised from the dead, never to suffer or die again (Heb 10:11 – 14; Rev 1:18). The very idea of rising refers primarily to his body. His spirit did not die; he commended it to his Father. So in the Bible the resurrection does not mean, as some suggest, that the spirit of Jesus lived on and was somehow available to his disciples after his death; it means his body was raised to life and in the completeness of his person Jesus came back to them (Mt 28:5 – 6; Lk 24:38 – 39; Jn 20:17, 24 – 29; 1 Cor 15:3 – 20).

Having given convincing evidence of his resurrection

to his disciples, and having taught them many things they could not grasp in earlier days (Acts 1:3), *in his resurrection body Jesus ascended into heaven* (Lk 24:50–51; Acts 1:9–11). Notice that he has not laid aside his human nature to return to heaven; in his body—raised, glorified, fitted for heaven (Phil 3:21; 1 Cor 15:43–49)—he has gone to the right hand of the Father *where he is exalted as Lord of all* (Mt 28:18; Eph 1:20–23; Phil 2:9–11).

Though the work of accomplishing salvation took place on earth and never needs to be repeated or added to at all, the Lord Jesus Christ still has a ministry on our behalf in heaven. *He intercedes for his people in the presence of the Father* (Heb 7:25). We should not think of this ministry in terms of pleading for our forgiveness—the Father needs no persuasion to continue forgiving us. Rather, the very appearance of Christ (Heb 9:24) as the One who offered the perfect sacrifice for our sins is the pledge and guarantee of our acceptance with God. Think of it! The Lamb who was slain for us is at the centre of the throne of heaven (Rev 5:6)!

Errors and heresies about the person and work of our Lord Jesus Christ are very serious (Jn 8:24; 2 Jn 7–9), and there are many of them. For this reason it is important that we read the Bible carefully, and hold firmly to the truths it reveals on this subject. We need to honour Christ, giving him his rightful place in our minds and hearts. We need also to be able to help inexperienced or confused believers and refute the errors to which they are exposed.

How wonderful is Jesus Christ; how amazing the grace he has shown to us! 'Simon,' said Jesus to Peter, 'do you love me?' 'Lord,' replied Peter, 'you know all things; you know that I love you' (Jn 21:17). Do you?

Study Questions

1. Make a list of all the verses you can find which demonstrate the deity of Christ. Learn the most important off by heart and keep the list for future reference.

2. Why do you think it is important to believe that Jesus was born of a virgin?

3. How does this statement show us that Jesus Christ is a prophet, priest and king?

4. How is the love of Jesus Christ shown us by his death and how does the cross show us the love of the Father too?

5. What difference does it make to us that Jesus was raised from the dead?

5

About Salvation

Salvation is entirely a work of God's grace and cannot be earned or deserved. It has been accomplished by the Lord Jesus Christ and is offered to all in the gospel. God in his love forgives sinners whom he calls, granting them repentance and faith. All who believe in Christ are justified by faith alone, adopted into the family of God and receive eternal life.

*   *   *

'What must I do to be saved?' (Acts 16:30) This question takes us right to the heart of the gospel. How is it that a person actually becomes a Christian and finds peace with God? The answer of biblical Christianity stands in stark contrast to the answers given by all the world's other religions. The first thing to grasp is that we cannot save ourselves (Mk 10:26–27). It is God himself who saves us (Rev 7:10), through his Son, our Lord Jesus Christ (Mt 1:21; Acts 4:12). *Salvation is entirely a work of God's grace* (Eph 2:5). We are not even to imagine that God graciously gives salvation in response to some good quality that he sees in us (Tit 3:5; 2 Tim 1:9). Salvation *cannot be earned or deserved* (Gal 2:16).

Our salvation does not rest on anything that is in us, but on what has *been accomplished by the Lord Jesus Christ* (Jn 3:17; Acts 15:11) in his death and resurrection (1 Cor 1:18; 2 Tim 1:9–10). This is of great importance. If our salvation ultimately depended on anything that we ourselves had done, we could never be sure that we had done it properly. We can be sure of our salvation, only because we are sure about our Lord Jesus Christ and are confident that his death is sufficient to take away all our sins. When Jesus died on the cross, he cried out triumphantly, 'It is finished' (Jn 19:30), indicating that the way of salvation was opened for all the people of God. It is this good news that is at the heart of the gospel. We are called to preach the triumph of the death and the resurrection of Jesus, and proclaim the salvation that God *offers to all in the gospel* (Rom 1:16).

God acts rightly and with justice when he forgives us, because he counts all our sins as having been taken by Christ (Rom 3:26). But we must never think of our salvation simply in terms of God's justice. God has chosen to save us because he loves us. The love of the Father is seen in his sending the Son to save sinners (Rom 5:8). The love of the Son is seen in laying down his life for us (Jn 15:13). We are saved because *God in his love forgives sinners* (Col 2:13).

The emphasis must be placed on God's forgiveness, because even as Christians we continually need to be forgiven. To be saved is not to be without sin (1 Jn 1:8). Every Christian knows from experience what it is to fail in many ways. The Christian has the great assurance that all his sins, conscious and unconscious, remembered and forgotten, past, present, and even future, have been taken by his Saviour, and therefore are forgiven by God

(1 Jn 2:1–2; Heb 10:17). The whole of our guilt and
sin has been taken by Christ and our salvation is
complete in him (Rom 8:1).

The Bible never suggests, however, that all sinners
are forgiven by God. It is quite clear that this forgiveness
only comes to those who belong to the Lord Jesus Christ
(Heb 2:3; Acts 4:12). How does this relationship come
about?

The first thing is that God calls us. This is essential
because the Bible makes it clear that in ourselves we are
blind to the truth of the gospel (2 Cor 4:4) and deaf to
the voice of God. In calling us, God wakes us up to our
own need and to the good news of the Lord Jesus Christ
(1 Pet 2:9; 5:10; Acts 2:39; Jude 1; 2 Thess 2:14).
Salvation, then, comes to *sinners whom he calls*. Bible-
believing Christians have different views about exactly
what is involved in this call, but all Christians have a
deep awareness that they have only got to where they
are because God has spoken to them, and drawn them
to the Saviour (Jn 6:44).

God not only calls sinners, but he also *grants them
repentance and faith* by which they turn from sin, to Christ,
and are saved (Acts 5:31; 11:18; Eph 2:8). Repentance
and faith must continue, develop and mature throughout
our Christan lives. Repentance may be described as
turning with as much as you know of yourself, from as
much as you know of sin, to as much as you know of
God. As our knowledge of self, sin and God grows
deeper, so will our repentance. Faith can be pictured
as a hand open to receive. It is not something that we
bring as a contribution to our salvation. On the contrary,
it is recognising that we have nothing to offer God, and
turning to trust and depend on him in everything. We
have faith in Christ when we have given up hoping in

ourselves, and have begun to trust him and look to him to give us all that we need to be saved.

Both faith and repentance must advance rather than diminish with the years. We cannot achieve this by ourselves. Repentance and faith are gifts and graces that God gives to us.

This then is how God saves us. God does it all, so that we are humbled, and can only thank him and give him all the praise and glory.

So what must *we* do to be saved? If it is God who calls us, and God who gives repentance and faith, then what is there left for us to do?

The Bible will never allow us to sit back passively and say that it is all up to God. The Bible calls on all men and women to believe in the Lord Jesus Christ (Acts 16:31), and offers the promise of salvation to all who believe (Jn 3:16). This believing is not just a mental assent, but a true persuasion about the Lord Jesus Christ that leads us to trust him fully.

All who believe in Christ are justified (Acts 13:39; Rom 1:16). This means not only that they are forgiven, but that they are reckoned righteous in the eyes of God himself (2 Cor 5:21; Rom 4:24). Of course we are not righteous because of the quality of our Christian lives, but because the perfect righteousness of Jesus Christ is counted as belonging to us (1 Cor 1:30).

Justification is *by faith alone* (Rom 3:28; Gal 3:11) because it is only by faith that we belong to Jesus Christ and only by belonging to him can we be right with God. We are not to imagine that our faith is the thing that saves. If that were the case we would always be worried about whether our faith was strong enough! It is Christ who saves, and he is always strong enough. That is our assurance. What this does mean is that faith is the only way in which God's salvation in Christ can be received. It cannot come to us without faith (Rom 1:17).

As believers in Jesus Christ, we also belong to the Christian family. We are no longer God's enemies but his friends. We are no longer alienated from him (Eph 2:19), but rather are *adopted into the family of God* and are all brothers and sisters in Christ (Jn 1:12; 1 Pet 2:10; 1 Jn 3:1).

Salvation does not end with our experience in this life. Together with our justification and adoption, God crowns his saving work by giving to all his people the gift of eternal life (Jn 3:15). In fact we *receive eternal life* as soon as we become Christians (1 Jn 5:11–12; Jn 10:10). Eternal life begins when we know Jesus Christ (Jn 17:3). But it is much more. Christ is preparing a place for us so that we will spend eternity with him in the glory that he now enjoys (Jn 14:2–3). When we see him our salvation will be complete (1 Jn 3:2). Then we will look back filled with unspeakable joy and gratitude to God for the love by which he saved us at the immeasurable cost of the death of his Son.

Study Questions

1. In what way is the Bible's teaching about salvation different from the teaching found in cult groups and other religions?
2. Why do many people reject the gospel? What can we do about this?
3. Why is it important to emphasise that we are justified by faith alone?
4. What is the relevance of eternal life to our Christian living now?
5. What should our response be to God's saving work in our lives?

6

About the Holy Spirit

The Holy Spirit has been sent from heaven to glorify Christ and to apply his work of salvation. He convicts sinners, imparts spiritual life and gives a true understanding of the Scriptures. He indwells all believers, brings assurance of salvation and produces increasing likeness to Christ. He builds up the Church and empowers its members for worship, service and mission.

*   *   *

The Holy Spirit is the third person of the Trinity and has been at work in the world since the creation (Gen 1:2). The Holy Spirit is not to be thought of as some mysterious, impersonal force or influence. He is 'he' not 'it'.

The Old Testament prophets looked forward to the time when the Messiah would come, for then the Spirit would be given in far greater measure (Is 11:2; 44:3; Joel 2:28 – 32). Today, Christians rejoice because *the Holy Spirit has been sent from heaven* by the Father and the Son to all believers (Jn 14:26; 15:26).

The Holy Spirit has no desire to be the centre of

attention. His task is *to glorify Christ* (Jn 16:14 – 15) *and to apply his work of salvation*. He is therefore happy to be called 'the Spirit of Jesus' (Acts 16:7) or 'the Spirit of Christ' (1 Pet 1:11) or 'the Spirit of [God's] Son' (Gal 4:6).

Because he brings the blessings of Christ's finished work into the lives of God's people, the Holy Spirit could not be poured out until the risen Saviour had ascended in triumph to be glorified at the Father's side (Jn 7:39; 16:7). But ever since the Day of Pentecost, the world has seen his miraculous working in people's lives.

He convicts sinners of guilt in regard to sin and righteousness and judgement (Jn 16:8). They are woken up by the Spirit to realise how they have grieved and offended a holy and loving God (Eph 5:14). The intensity of these spiritual convictions varies enormously but they must be real enough to cause the sinner to seek the Saviour (Lk 15:15 – 20; Acts 2:37; 16:29 – 30). These are the first outward signs of that miracle of grace by which the Holy Spirit *imparts spiritual life*.

Spiritually we are dead in our transgressions and sins (Eph 2:1) until we are born again by the Spirit (Jn 3:1 – 8). By this wonderful act of God, the sinner becomes 'a new creation' (2 Cor 5:17) and receives a new nature with new spiritual interests, values, motives, tastes, desires, hopes, priorities and goals (Eph 4:22 – 24). The Christian life is then lived entirely in the power of the Spirit (Rom 8:1 – 17).

None of the Spirit's work in the lives of believers would be possible apart from the word of God (Jn 17:17). The Bible is his supreme instrument, his 'sword' (Eph 6:17). It is not surprising therefore to discover that the Spirit, who in fact brought the Scriptures into being (2 Pet 1:21), should also interpret its meaning. He *gives a true understanding of the Scriptures*. How dull the Bible often appears to the unbeliever! He cannot make head nor tail of it. It is 'foolishness' to him. But the Spirit opens the eyes, ears and minds of Christians so that they may understand what God has freely given them (1 Cor 2:6–16). It is the Spirit who causes us to love the word of God, so we can be sure that anything which causes us to neglect it does not come from him.

Having saved us, God puts his Spirit in our hearts (2 Cor 1:22), so that we can say *he indwells all believers*. If anyone does not have the Spirit of Christ, he does not belong to Christ (Rom 8:9). The body of every Christian is therefore a temple of the Holy Spirit (1 Cor 6:19). This is a staggering truth—God is in you! When believers are truly possessed and controlled by the Spirit within, and at times when the Spirit comes particularly upon his people, they are described as being 'full of' or 'filled with' the Spirit (Lk 1:41,67; Acts 2:4; 4:8,31; 6:3,5; 7:55; 9:17; 11:24; 13:9). The Apostle Paul told all the members of the church in Ephesus literally to 'go on being filled with the Spirit' (Eph 5:18). This is the experience of all who long for God and truly seek to serve him (Is 44:3; Jn 4:15).

Some Christians seem to drift through life uncertain as to whether they are really saved or not. This is a great coup of the devil, the 'accuser' (Rev 12:10), who loves to rob us of our peace, joy and usefulness. One book of the New Testament, the first letter of John, was written expressly for the purpose of assuring believers that they have eternal life (1 Jn 5:13). John tells us that it is the Holy Spirit who *brings assurance of salvation* (1 Jn 3:24; 4:13).

As we read the Scriptures, the Spirit convinces us that the promises of the gospel have not failed us. We read, further, that he has 'sealed' us, a word that speaks of our guaranteed security as the precious property of God (2 Cor 1:22; Eph 1:13; 4:30). As he works in our lives, we can see the beginnings of the 'marks of grace' that are evidence of God's saving work (1 Jn 2:29; 3:9; 4:7; 5:1,4). All in all, he longs to grant us the inner certainty that we are the children of God (Rom 8:16).

Because he is the Holy Spirit, his principal influence on our lives is to make us holy. This process is known as sanctification. It begins at conversion and will not be completed until we enter heaven. Sanctification is the work of the Spirit in believers which *produces increasing likeness to Christ* (2 Cor 3:17 – 18). By his power we are able to put to death the sins which have often controlled us (Rom 8:13). On the positive side, every evidence of holy living is described as 'the fruit of the Spirit' (Gal 5:22 – 26). He is constantly battling within us against the remnants of our old sinful nature (Gal 5:17 – 18), but the victory is certain for those who earnestly endeavour to please God (Phil 2:12 – 13; Rom 7:24 – 25). One day our likeness to Christ will be complete (1 Jn 3:2).

All the Spirit's gifts are given for the common good of God's people. He baptises us into Christ's body, the Church (1 Cor 12:13), so that in mutual dependence on one another we each play our part as we share our various gifts and graces (Rom 12:3 – 8). In this way the Spirit *builds up the Church* (Eph 4:1 – 16). All he gives us is for the growth of the Church and never for mere selfish indulgence. So we are built together to become a dwelling in which God lives by his Spirit (Eph 2:22).

Every ministry of the Church is utterly dependent upon the presence and working of the Holy Spirit. He *empowers its members for worship*. God is spirit and his worshippers must worship in spirit and in truth (Jn 4:24).

Consequently, the only aid to worship we require and the only aid we should desire is the Holy Spirit himself (Phil 3:3). By him we pray (Rom 8:15; Eph 6:18; Jude 20), preach (1 Cor 2:4) and sing God's praises (Eph 5:18–20).

The Spirit also empowers the members of Christ's body for *service and mission*. Everything the Apostle Paul accomplished in his service to God he attributed to the power of the Spirit (Rom 15:17–19). Primarily he had in mind the success of his missionary endeavours. The Holy Spirit was originally given at Pentecost to empower the apostles to be Christ's witnesses to the ends of the earth (Acts 1:8), a commission and a task in which we all share. We depend on the same Holy Spirit for power as we witness to our family and friends. This gives us great encouragement, not only to reach out to the lost but also to watch and pray for that time when the Lord will again pour out his Spirit upon us in true revival.

Study Questions

1. 'Christians today are obsessed with the Holy Spirit when the Holy Spirit wants us to be obsessed with Jesus Christ.' What comments would you make on this statement?
2. How can we obey the command to be filled with the Holy Spirit (Eph 5:18)?
3. To what extent, according to the Bible, does sanctification depend on our efforts?
4. How would you help a young believer who lacks assurance of salvation?
5. If the Bible does not speak to us apart from the Holy Spirit, does the Holy Spirit speak to us apart from the Bible? What objections could be raised to your answer?

7

About the Church

The universal Church is the body of which Christ is the head and to which all who are saved belong. It is made visible in local churches, which are congregations of believers who are committed to each other for the worship of God, the preaching of the word, the administering of baptism and the Lord's Supper, for pastoral care and discipline, and for evangelism. The unity of the body of Christ is expressed within and between churches by mutual love, care and encouragement. True fellowship between churches exists only where they are faithful to the gospel.

*   *   *

Christ gave himself for the Church (Eph 5:25). We are often so concerned to emphasise God's love and plans for the individual, that we can fail to give due weight to God's love for his people and his great plan for them as a living unity.

The starting point in our understanding must be that *the universal church is the body of which Christ is the head and to which all who are saved belong*. Scripture uses the word 'church' to include all God's people of every age and every place (Mt 16:18; Eph 5:23 – 32). It will never be gathered together in this world, but it will be seen in glory as the Church triumphant (Rev 7:9 – 10).

Scripture gives us various pictures of the church to help our understanding. It is a spiritual house (Eph 2:21 – 22; 1 Pet 2:5); it is the bride of Christ (Eph 5:25; Rev 19:7). But supremely the Church is the body of Christ (Col 1:18; Eph 1:22 – 23). It is living, active, growing, organically united but full of amazing variety. All who are alive in Christ are members of his body. All who are saved belong to the universal Church. We cannot belong unless we are saved. We cannot be saved and not belong.

The universal Church *is made visible in local churches*. Wherever 'church' is not used to describe the universal Church it refers to local churches. The letters of Paul are sent to local churches. The seven churches in Revelation 2 – 3 are local churches. Such churches in New Testament times and in the present day express the reality of the universal Church and make it visible here and now.

It is important to be clear at this point that Scripture does not allow us to speak about the Church in a national or denominational sense. This means that local churches are independent of external control or any form of central government. Churches may well associate with each other for fellowship, but this does not involve surrendering their independence nor their self-government under Christ as their head.

So what are local churches? They are *congregations of believers who are committed to each other*. Although anyone of any religion or of none at all is welcome to come into our church buildings and attend our services, the local church, just like the universal Church, is made up of believers only (1 Cor 1:2). These believers are not simply individual Christians who happen to meet in the same building; they are called by God to be united together in true fellowship within the spiritual family of the local church (Acts 2:42–47). They are *committed to each other for the worship of God* (Acts 4:24–31; 13:2), for *the preaching of the word* (Acts 20:7; Eph 4:11; 2 Tim 4:2), for *the administering of baptism* (Acts 8:12; 18:8; 19:5), *and the Lord's Supper* (Acts 2:42; 1 Cor 11:18–28), *for pastoral care and discipline* (1 Pet 5:2–3; Mt 18:17; 2 Thess 3:6), and *for evangelism* (Acts 2:47).

The local church rather than parachurch organisations is the true setting for these activities, all of which are to be an expression of the life of the Holy Spirit in the church, as his gifts to the body are exercised (Rom 12:3–8; 1 Cor 12:7–11). The local church must never be thought of in terms of one 'omni-competent' minister and a passive membership, but as an active team in which all have their gift, calling and ministry. For this reason all members, together with duly appointed officers (1 Tim 3:1–13; 5:17–18), must share in responsibility for and support of the local church (Acts 6:3).

In the New Testament local churches related to each other. Scripture teaches independence but prohibits isolationism. *The unity of the body of Christ is expressed within and between churches by mutual love, care and encouragement.* There is to be unity between Christians within a local church. This is far from easy, but the New Testament consistently teaches the spiritual basis for unity (1 Cor 3:5–9; Eph 2:11–22), and encourages Christians to preserve and promote that unity (Eph 4:1–6; Phil 2:1–11). Every believer should be actively involved in the growth of love, peace and unity in the local church.

It is no less important that there should be unity

between churches. Independence is to be balanced by interdependence. In the New Testament, churches were kept informed about each other's problems and progress (1 Thess 2:14). They acted to help each other in times of need: the obvious example is the 'contribution for the poor among the saints in Jerusalem' (Rom 15:26; Acts 11:29–30; 1 Cor 16:1–4). The New Testament letters were circulated (Col 4:16). Ministries were shared for the benefit of the churches (2 Cor 8:18). The churches were encouraged by each other's example (1 Thess 1:7). They sent greetings to each other (Rom 16:16; 1 Cor 16:19–20). Members of one church who had to travel or move were commended to other churches (Rom 16:1–2). Obviously the fellowship between churches was very real and precious to them.

It must also be recognised that *true fellowship between churches exists only where they are faithful to the gospel*. The basis for church unity is not mere profession of the name Christian, nor membership in a denomination, but faithfulness to Jesus Christ and to the fundamentals of the gospel (Gal 1:8–9; 2 Cor 6:14–18).

However much it is ridiculed, despised or persecuted throughout history, the destiny of the church of Jesus Christ is final triumph, perfection and glory (Eph 5:25–27; Mt 24:31; Rev 19:6–9). Till that day we should count it a very great privilege to belong to the Church and put our prayer and service into making our own local church the best it can be for the glory of our Lord Jesus Christ, the head of the Church.

Study Questions

1. What special truths are emphasised by the different New Testament pictures of the universal Church?
2. What do you think should be the requirements for membership of a local church?
3. What are the particular dangers for a church that takes an isolated position?
4. What do churches need to agree on before they can work together?
5. What can we learn from the New Testament that will strengthen fellowship between churches?

8

About Baptism and the Lord's Supper

Baptism and the Lord's Supper have been given to the churches by Christ as visible signs of the gospel. Baptism is a symbol of union with Christ and entry into his church but does not impart spiritual life. The Lord's Supper is a commemoration of Christ's sacrifice offered once for all and involves no change in the bread and wine. All its blessings are received by faith.

*　　*　　*

Before our Lord Jesus Christ ascended into heaven, he gave clear instructions regarding the place that Baptism and the Lord's Supper was to have in the life of the church. In the great commission, the twelve were told to baptise disciples from all nations in the name of the Father and the Son and the Holy Spirit (Mt 28:19). At the Last Supper, Christ made it clear that the disciples were to renew their fellowship with him regularly in the breaking of bread (Lk 22:19; 1 Cor 11:23–26). So *Baptism and the Lord's Supper were given to the churches by Christ*. This is why they are of great importance in the Christian life. Every Christian should be baptised, and every Christian should regularly share in the Lord's

Supper. These are not optional extras for enthusiastic believers; they are gifts and commands of our Lord himself.

It is not surprising then that these things were established right at the very beginning of the church on the Day of Pentecost, when over 3,000 were baptised (Acts 2:41) and then gave themselves to the apostles' teaching, the fellowship, the breaking of bread and prayer (Acts 2:42,46). Wherever the gospel spread, Baptism and the Lord's Supper were observed and established (Acts 8:12,36–38; 9:17–18; 10:44–48; 16:14–15, 31–33; 18:8; 20:7) and therefore these things served as a focus of the unity of the Church (Eph 4:4; 1 Cor 10:17).

It is one of the great tragedies of the history of the Church, that Baptism and the Lord's Supper have become such a focus of confusion, misunderstanding and division. Too often these wonderful gifts of Christ are surrounded by superstition, instead of being approached with faith. Our statement emphasises the things on which all Bible-believing Christians are united, and specifically denies some views of Baptism and the Lord's Supper that are clearly contrary to Scripture.

As well as speaking to us through the words of Scripture, God also speaks visually through Baptism and the Lord's Supper. They are *visible signs of the gospel*, centering our thoughts on what Christ has done for us. Baptism depicts the washing or cleansing that is at the heart of becoming a Christian (Acts 22:16; 1 Cor 6:11; 1 Pet 3:21; Heb 10:22; Eph 5:26). The Lord's Supper depicts the feeding and nourishing that we continually need and that we receive from Christ who was crucified for us (Jn 6:57–58).

Baptism is a symbol of union with Christ. It is by faith that we are joined to Jesus Christ (Gal 2:20), but Baptism is a wonderful demonstration of what is involved in that relationship. Just as Jesus Christ has died and risen, so every Christian has died and risen (Rom 6:3–4). The old life has died, ended and been buried (Rom 6:6). A new life of faith, love and service has begun (Rom 6:4). Christ makes the Christian a new person (2 Cor 5:17). All of this is powerfully symbolised in Baptism.

To be a Christian is a deeply personal thing, but it is more than that; to belong to Christ is to belong to the body of Christ, the church. Christians rejoice to see others baptised, not only because they have been brought to Christ, but also because in Baptism there is a recognition that we belong to one another. In this way Baptism is a symbol of *entry into Christ's Church* (1 Cor 12:12–13).

There are of course differences of emphasis, understanding and practice among Bible-believing Christians with regard to Baptism. These differences are important, but they are not the most important thing. All evangelical churches, whether they baptise infants or believers, affirm that Baptism *does not impart spiritual life*. We can never experience a spiritual change of heart simply by being baptised. Apart from faith, Baptism is meaningless and empty. Bible churches that baptise infants acknowledge that the infant needs to come to faith in Christ for salvation. Those churches that baptise believers acknowledge that this only has significance where there is already faith in Christ (Mk 16:16).

For a right understanding of the Lord's Supper, faith is again the key. *The Lord's Supper is a commemoration of Christ's sacrifice*. The supper involves us looking back in history to the death of our Lord Jesus Christ (1 Cor 11:24–25). This is of great importance. Christian faith is based on unchangeable facts. Christ died. Christ bore our sins. Christ rose (1 Cor 15:3–5; 1 Pet 2:24). In these things there is certain proof of the love of God for us (Rom 5:8). The Lord's Supper enriches our Christian lives because in a special way it focuses our minds and hearts on the Saviour and all that he has accomplished for us at Calvary. As we think about these things with faith, our hearts are encouraged and strengthened (Jn 6:57–58).

Through the centuries many churches have fallen into serious errors about the Lord's Supper. Some think that the communion service is like another sacrifice for sin. This is totally wrong. There is nothing in the Lord's Supper which saves us. Christ's sacrifice was *offered once for all*. It can never by repeated (Heb 9:25–28): it does not need to be repeated (Heb 10:11–12). Faith constantly looks back to the miracle of our salvation. The Lord's Supper points us back to the cross which is the only place where sin has been taken away (Is 53:4–6).

Some think that in the communion service, there is some change in the bread and the wine, so that instead of simply representing Christ's sacrifice to us, they actually become the body and blood of Christ which we then eat and drink. Again, this is totally wrong. The Lord's Supper *involves no change in the bread and wine*. The bread and wine are symbols, they remain what they are. It is not the symbol that is important but the thing that is symbolised. When we receive the bread and the wine, our minds and our hearts are to be led to Christ crucified and risen, in worship, thanksgiving, faith, hope and love.

When we understand the Lord's Supper in this way, it becomes clear that *all its blessings are received by faith*. There is nothing magical here. The bread and wine are only of value to those who believe. Where there is faith, however, the Lord's Supper is something very precious indeed. At the communion service there is a special fulfilment of God's promise that as we draw near to him, he will draw near to us (Jas 4:8). There are great blessings for believers every time we draw near to our Saviour in thanksgiving for his body broken and his blood shed for us. At the Lord's table we are reminded of our unity as one body in Christ and assured of the forgiveness of our sins. Faith and love are strengthened and we look forward to Christ's return.

Study Questions

1. What do you understand by the phrase 'union with Christ'?
2. Why is Baptism important?
3. How should we use a time of quiet during a communion service?
4. Why have Baptism and the Lord's Supper been the source of so many problems and disagreements in the history of the church?
5. Why is faith so important in coming to the Lord's Supper? Are there other things that are also important as we come to the Lord's table? (Look up 1 Corinthians 11:28 and Matthew 5:23–24.)

9

About the Future

The Lord Jesus Christ will return in glory. He will raise the dead and judge the world in righteousness. The wicked will be sent to eternal punishment and the righteous will be welcomed into a life of eternal joy in fellowship with God. God will make all things new and will be glorified for ever.

*　　*　　*

The Christian Church is a community full of confident and living hope (1 Pet 1:3). However involved in this world its members may have to be, there is always before them the certainty that *the Lord Jesus Christ will return*. The time of his return is unknown to the Church on earth (Mt 24:36) and there will be no immediate warning of his coming (Mt 24:42). We should distrust and can ignore those who claim to predict the date of our Lord's return (Mt 24:23 – 24); they have always been wrong in the past and will always be wrong in the future.

On some details of the return of Christ the Scriptures do not give us information; on other matters the Bible is very precise. We should not allow ourselves to become intolerant of those who hold different views from ours about the order of events surrounding Christ's coming (often referred to as millennial views), or about the details of judgement and heaven. The fact that Christ will come *in glory* is part of our great expectation. This does not only mean that he will come with a brilliant light surrounding him, though that is likely (Mt 24:27), but that he will appear in all his beauty, holiness, power and perfection. He will be seen as he really is (1 Jn 3:2); that is glory.

On that awesome day *he will raise the dead and judge the world*. All the dead will be raised, both believers and unbelievers, and that will be a literal, physical resurrection. When the dead have been raised, Christians alive at his coming will be carried up to meet Christ (1 Thess 4:16 – 17). All this is a great mystery to us, but not to the God with whom everything is possible.

Then will follow the judgement. All will be judged, both Christian and non-Christian; but Christians need have no fear of the final sentence. Our salvation is secured by Christ, not by our own good works; so no sin can be laid against the Christian to condemn him (Rom 8:1) and he can never be separated from Christ (Rom 8:35 – 39). What Christians will face is a test of the quality of the life they have lived for God. Although our salvation will be secure, there will be rewards to be gained or lost, such as the commendation of our Saviour and the satisfaction of a life wisely lived for him. Sadly, some Christians will have nothing of lasting value to offer their Lord on that day (1 Cor 3:12 – 15).

Unbelievers will also be judged and that judgement will be a terrifying thing. The secrets of men will be exposed (Rom 2:16) and the sinfulness of their hearts and lives will silence any excuse that may be put forward (Rom 3:19 – 20). The wicked will long to hide from the judgement of God and of Christ but they will find nowhere to escape (Rev 6:15 – 17). All God's judgements will be *in righteousness* so that both believer and unbeliever will acknowledge the justice and fairness of God's verdict and sentence. There will be nothing unjust in God's judgements.

At the end of time *the wicked will be sent to eternal punishment*. The word 'punishment' that our Lord himself uses (in Matthew 25:46, for example) is a word that always means a conscious suffering; and 'eternal' refers to something that goes on for ever and ever (Rev 20:10). We should not think of physical torment alone, but the terrible remorse of opportunities lost and the aweful experience of separation from God himself.

This is a terrifying prospect. So terrifying, in fact, that there are some Christians who are tempted to avoid the plain meaning of the Bible. Some claim that unbelievers are blotted out into oblivion, or nothingness, immediately at death. Others say that unbelievers, when raised from the dead, will face the anger of God's judgement for a period, and then be sent into oblivion where they do not feel or know anything ever again. This is known as 'conditional immortality' or 'annihilation'. But we cannot change the plain meaning of the Scriptures just because we find eternal punishment emotionally unacceptable. 'Eternal', whether used of heaven or hell, means for ever and ever, and 'punishment' means conscious awareness and suffering; in the Bible 'death' never refers to annihilation.

The Bible is full of promises God gives to those who are declared righteous through faith in Jesus Christ. *The righteous will be welcomed into a life of eternal joy in fellowship with God*. Since our greatest goal is to know God (Eph 1:17), our greatest joy must be to remain in unbroken friendship with him for ever. Peter writes of Christians receiving a 'rich welcome into the eternal kingdom of our Lord and Saviour Jesus Christ' (2 Pet 1:11), and the privilege not merely of entering heaven, but of being 'welcomed' into heaven by the Father and Son is unimaginable!

Finally, *God will make all things new*. He will create a new heaven and a new earth, the home of righteousness (2 Pet 3:13; Rev 21:1). We cannot expect to understand the details of this or the nature of our life in heaven. It will be all so different and it will so surpass our present knowledge and thinking, that the Bible can only describe heaven as the place where God is (Ezek 48:35; Rev 21:3; 22:4–5)—and that is enough! The triune God *will be glorified for ever* so that his beauty and holiness will be known in all its splendour and he will be given the honour due to his name (1 Cor 15:28; Rev 5:13–14).

Study Questions

1. What answer would you give to those who scorn the return of Christ as something Christians have always hoped for, but that never happens?
2. What will be the reason for the final punishment of unbelievers?
3. What arguments are used against the teaching that eternal punishment is conscious suffering for ever and ever, and how would you reply to them?
4. What are the blessings of eternal life?
5. In what way does our future hope help us to live the Christian life now?